WHS

LAST MINUTE REVISION

GCSE
FRENCH
Booster

First published 2000
exclusively for WHSmith by

Hodder & Stoughton Educational
338 Euston Road
London NW1 3BH

Text and illustrations © Hodder & Stoughton Educational 2000

All rights reserved. No part of this publication may be reproduced or transmitted in any form or by any means, electronic or mechanical, including photocopying, recording or any information storage and retrieval system, without permission in writing from the publisher.

A CIP record for this book is available from the British Library.

Text: Philippa Lyons
Developed and edited by Hart McLeod

ISBN 0340 780886
Printed and bound by Hobbs The Printers, Totton, Hants

Calais

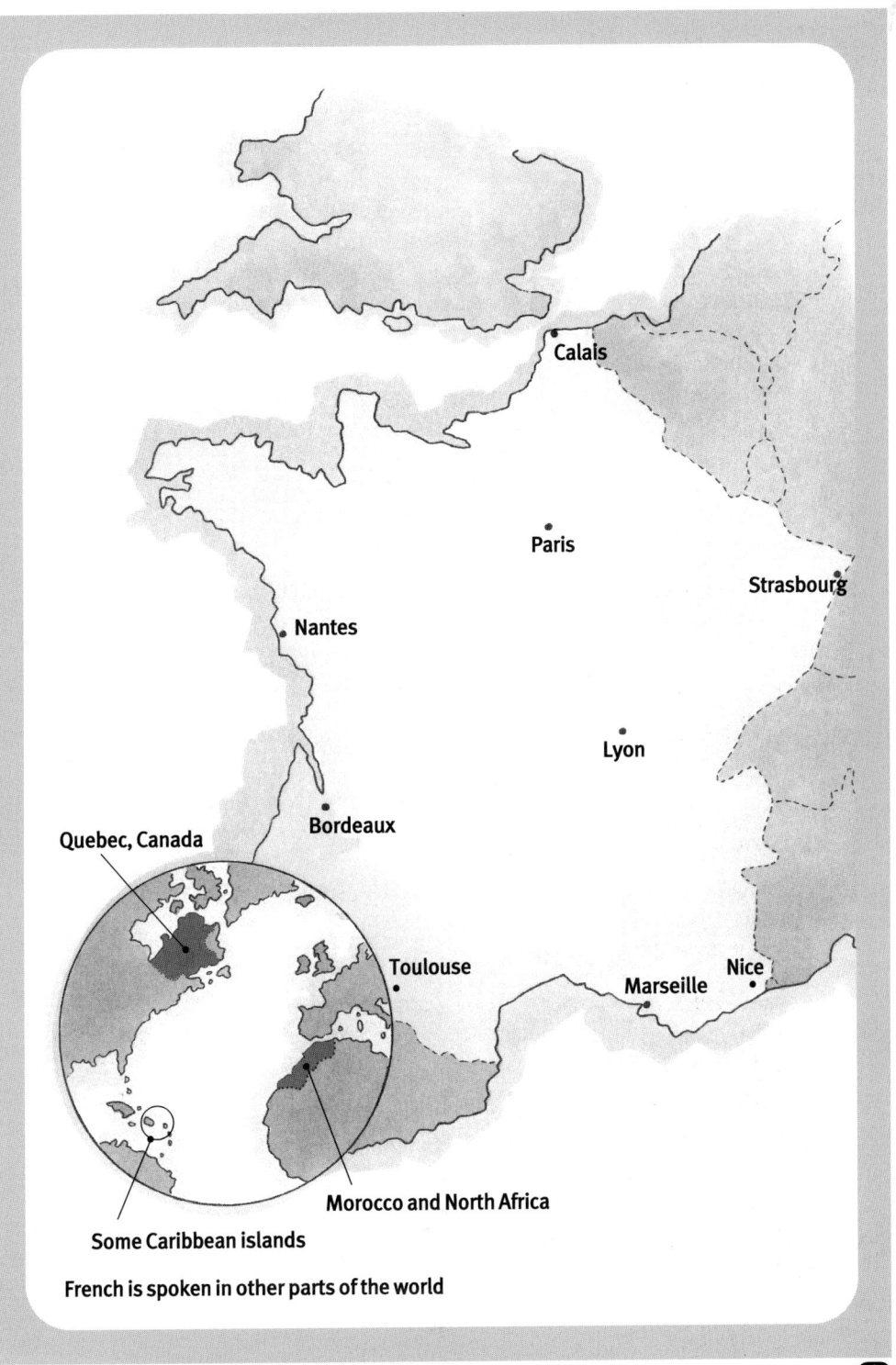

Paris

Strasbourg

Nantes

Lyon

Bordeaux

Quebec, Canada

Toulouse

Marseille

Nice

Morocco and North Africa

Some Caribbean islands

French is spoken in other parts of the world

Accents

French has five of these. This one (¨) is very rare, but the other four are much more common.
- **The acute accent** (´) only ever goes over an **e**. This is the really important one, as it goes over the last **e** in the past participles of regular **er** verbs. Make sure you remember to use it!
- **The grave accent** (`) goes over an **e** as well, and in the words **à** (to) and **où** (where).
- **The circumflex** (^) can go over any vowel. (It usually means that there used to be an **s** there in old French spelling.)
- **The cedilla** (¸) goes under a **c** to give it an **s** sound when it's followed by a hard vowel (a, o, u).

Exam tip

Accents are part of spelling, so they do count, especially the acute accent. They are hardly ever used over capital letters these days.

Adjectives

Position of adjectives

Most adjectives come **after** the noun, including all the adjectives of colour. However, some very common adjectives come **in front of** the noun, like they do in English. Here are the most common ones.

grand (*big/tall*)	bon (*good*)	nouveau (*new*)	joli (*attractive*)
petit (*small*)	mauvais (*bad*)	vieux (*old*)	gros (*big/fat*)
beau (*beautiful*)	haut (*high*)		

Adjectives have to **match the nouns they describe**. This means that the endings may change according to whether the noun is masculine, feminine, singular or plural (see **Agreement**, page 3).

See also

Possessive adjectives, Comparison, Agreement

Adverbs

Most French adverbs are made by adding —ment to the **feminine** form of an adjective (see **Agreement**). This is like adding —ly to an adjective in English.
  parfait (m.) → parfait<u>e</u> (f.) + —ment = parfaitement (*perfectly*)

This works for **irregular adjectives** too.
  heureux (m.) → heureuse (f.) + —ment = heureusement (*luckily/happily*)

Exceptions to this rule are adjectives which end in **i** or **u**. Here, the —ment is added to the **masculine** form.
  poli (m.) + —ment = poliment (*politely*); vrai (m.) + —ment = vraiment (*really*); absolu (m.) + —ment = absolument (*absolutely*)

Some very common adverbs look nothing like their corresponding adjectives. You'll probably recognise these, but you still need to learn them!

  bien (*well*)   mal (*badly*)   mieux (*better*)
  vite (*quickly*)   peu (*little*)

See also Comparison

Agreement

Adjectives have to match (**agree with**) the noun they describe. This means that the ending of an adjective can change depending on whether the noun is masculine, feminine, singular or plural.

To make an adjective **feminine**, add **e** to the masculine form.

  grand grand**e** (*big/tall*)   fatigué fatigué**e** (*tired*)

Sometimes you double the final consonant before adding **e**.

  violet viole**tte** (*purple*)   gros gros**se** (*big/fat*)

Adjectives that already end in **e** stay as they are.

  jeune (*young*)   mince (*slim*)   rouge (*red*)   difficile (*difficult*)

See also Adjectives

Continued overleaf

Irregular adjectives

Adjectives ending in **f** change to **v** in the feminine, and those ending in **x** change to **s**.

sportif (m.) sportive (f.) (*sporty*)
neuf (m.) neuve (f.) (*new*)

heureux (m.) heureuse (f.) (*happy*)
affreux (m.) affreuse (f.) (*awful*)

Here are some other irregular adjectives that you should learn.

beau (m.) belle (f.) (*beautiful*)
doux (m.) douce (f.) (*sweet/soft*)

vieux (m.) vieille (f.) (*old*)
nouveau (m.) nouvelle (f.) (*new*)

Plural adjectives

Add **s** to the singular form of the adjective (m. or f.) for the plural.

le grand garçon (sing.)
la grande fille (sing.)

les grand**s** garçons (pl.)
les grand**es** filles (pl.)

Singular adjectives that already end in **s** or **x** stay as they are.

le gros chien (sing.)
un film ennuyeux (sing.)

les gros chiens (pl.)
des films ennuyeux (pl.)

Past participle agreement

Remember that when a verb takes *être* in the perfect tense, the past participle behaves like an adjective and **has to agree with the subject**.

Elle est resté**e** à la maison.
Ils sont reven**us** en France.
Elles sont mont**ées** dans le train.

She stayed at home.
They (m.) came back to France.
They (f.) got on the train.

- Watch out for 3rd person subjects (sing. or plu.) as nouns!

Mes parents sont partis au Portugal. *My parents left for Portugal.*

- Take care also when the subject is **je** or **nous**.

Je suis rentré(**e**) (m. or f.) hier.
Nous sommes allé(**e**)s (m. or f.) au café.

I came back yesterday.
We went to the café.

Animals

Pets

un chat (*cat*)
un cochon d'Inde (*guinea pig*)
une perruche (*budgie*)
un chien (*dog*)
un cheval (pl. chevaux) (*horse*)
un oiseau (pl. oiseaux) (*bird*)
un lapin (*rabbit*)
une tortue (*tortoise*)
un serpent (*snake*)
un hamster (*hamster*)
une souris (*mouse*)
une tortue d'eau (*terrapin*)

Farm animals

une vache (*cow*)
un cochon (*pig*)
une poule (*hen*)
un taureau (*bull*)
un mouton (*sheep*)
une chèvre (*goat*)
un agneau (*lamb*)
un âne (*donkey*)
un canard (*duck*)

Wild animals (the zoo)

un lion (*lion*)
un ours (*bear*)
un singe (*monkey*)
un tigre (*tiger*)

Appearance

Size and shape

You need the verb ***être*** when talking about these.

Je suis ... (assez, très)		I am ... (quite/fairly, very)	
	grand		tall, big
	petit		small
	mince		slim
	gros		fat, big
	joli		pretty
	laid		ugly
	beau		beautiful
	bronzé		tanned
	de taille moyenne		of average height

Continued overleaf

Hair and eyes

You need the verb *avoir* when talking about these.

J'ai ...	les cheveux	blonds	I have blonde hair
		châtain*	(*dark/light*)
		(foncé/clair)	brown/chestnut
		noirs	black
		roux	red
		gris	grey
		blancs	white
(assez/très)		longs (*quite/very*)	long
		courts	short
		raides	straight
		bouclés	curly/wavy
		ondulés	wavy
		frisés	very curly
		en brosse	spikey
Il a les yeux ...		bleus	He has blue eyes
		gris	grey
		noirs	black
		verts	green
		bleus-verts	bluey-green
		marron*	brown
		noisette*	hazel

Exam tip

Remember to make all adjectives agree!

except *châtain*, *marron*, *noisette*. These are not really adjectives at all (although they are used as such), so they don't need to agree.

Also useful are:

une barbe	a beard	je porte	I wear
des lunettes	glasses	– des lunettes	glasses
une moustache	a moustache	– des verres de contact	contact lenses

See also

Adjectives, Agreement

Avoir expressions

The verb *avoir* is probably the most useful verb of all, so you need to learn it thoroughly. As well as being a common verb in its own right (to have), it's used to form the **perfect tense** in French. It also crops up in the following very common expressions:

j'ai chaud	*I'm hot*	j'ai faim	*I'm hungry*
j'ai peur	*I'm afraid*	j'ai mal	*I'm hurt*
j'ai froid	*I'm cold*	j'ai soif	*I'm thirsty*
j'ai (seize) ans	*I'm (sixteen) years old*		

Exam tip

Be careful! In these expressions, *j'ai* is the equivalent of *I am* in English. Don't fall into the trap of translating it back into French using the verb *être*!

See also
Verbs – general

Body

Parts of the body

la tête	*head*	les oreilles (f.)	*ears*
les cheveux	*hair*	les dents (f.)	*teeth*
le dos	*back*	le coude	*elbow*
le derrière	*backside*	le pied	*foot*
le visage	*face*	le nez	*nose*
le cou	*neck*	les épaules (f.)	*shoulders*
le ventre	*stomach*	la main	*hand*
la jambe	*leg*	le cœur	*heart*
les yeux	*eyes*	la bouche	*mouth*
la gorge	*throat*	la poitrine	*chest*
le bras	*arm*	le doigt	*finger*
le genou	*knee*	le sang	*blood*

See also
Health

Cinema

Types of film

un film comique	a comedy
un film de science-fiction	a sci-fi film
un film d'épouvante	a horror film
un film policier	a detective film
un film d'aventures	an adventure
un film d'amour	a romance
un film à suspense	a thriller
un dessin animé	a cartoon

Also useful:

la séance	*(film) showing*
la vedette	*filmstar*

Clothes

la chemise	*shirt*	le chemisier	*blouse*
le jean	*jeans*	le short	*shorts*
le pull (over)	*jumper*	la robe	*dress*
les bottes (f.)	*boots*	la veste	*jacket*
les gants (m.)	*gloves*	le pyjama	*pyjamas*
le collant	*pair of tights*	les baskets (m.)	*trainers*
le sweat	*sweatshirt*	le tee-shirt	*T-shirt*
le pantalon	*trousers*	le jogging	*tracksuit*
la jupe	*skirt*	le gilet	*waistcoat*
les sandales (f.)	*sandals*	le manteau	*coat*
l'écharpe (f.)	*scarf*	la ceinture	*belt*
les chaussettes (f.)	*socks*		
les chaussures (f.)	*shoes*		
le maillot de bain	*swimming costume*		

Also useful:

le cuir	*leather*	le coton	*cotton*	la laine	*wool*

Colour

rouge	red	vert/verte	green
noir	black	blanc/blanche	white
bleu-marine	navy	bleu	blue
orange	orange	violet/violette	purple
gris/grise	grey	jaune	yellow
rose	pink	marron*	brown

Also useful:

clair	light	(bleu-clair	light blue)
foncé	dark	(vert-foncé	dark green)

Exam tip

Remember! Colours are adjectives and must agree with the noun they describe. *Not marron*, which isn't really an adjective at all.

See also Adjectives

Comparison

To compare two things, you use **plus** (more) or **moins** (less) with an adjective.

Sandrine est petite.	Sandrine is small.
Louise est **plus petite**.	Louise is smaller.
Le jean est cher.	The jeans are expensive.
Le short est **moins cher**.	The shorts are less expensive/cheaper.

Plus is like *–er* in English. Plus grand (*bigger*), plus facile (*easier*).

Exam tip

Remember to make the adjective agree with the noun it describes! Use *que* (than) when comparing two things in the same sentence. Il est plus marrant que son frère. (*He is funnier than his brother.*)

See also Adjectives

Conditional tense

You've probably been using this for a long time without realising it with the phrase *Je voudrais* (I would like) (see **Shopping**). Use this tense when you want to say what you **would** do (if you won the Lottery, for example!)

Here is the formula:

future stem	+	imperfect ending	=	conditional tense
j' aimer–	+	ais	=	j'aimerais (*I would like*)

Useful conditional phrases to learn:

je serais (*I would be*)   j'aurais (*I would have*)   je pourrais (*I could*)
j'irais (*I would go*)   je ferais (*I would do*)   je devrais (*I should*)
je dirais (*I should say*)   j'achèterais (*I would buy*)

and, of course, je voudrais (*I would like [to buy]*)

Countries

European

l'Angleterre (f.)	*England*	l'Ecosse (f.)	*Scotland*
la Belgique	*Belgium*	l'Allemagne (f.)	*Germany*
l'Italie (f.)	*Italy*	le Portugal	*Portugal*
la Norvège	*Norway*	la Grèce	*Greece*
le Pays de Galles	*Wales*	l'Irlande (f.)	*Irish Republic*
la France	*France*	le Luxembourg	*Luxembourg*
la Suisse	*Switzerland*	l'Espagne (f.)	*Spain*
la Suède	*Sweden*	les Pays Bas (m.)	*Netherlands*
l'Irlande (f.) du Nord	*Northern Ireland*	la Turquie	*Turkey*

Other countries

l'Australie (f.)	*Australia*	le Canada	*Canada*
la Nouvelle-Zélande	*New Zealand*	les Etats-Unis	*United States*

Saying *in* or *to* a country

- If a country is **feminine** (most of them are), use *en*
  en Angleterre (*in/to England*)   en Espagne (*in/to Spain*)
- If a country is **masculine**, use *au*
  au Pays de Galles (*in/to Wales*)   au Canada (*in/to Canada*)
- If a country is **plural** (very few of these), use *aux*
  aux Etats-Unis (*in/to the United States*)

See also Nationality

Daily routine

je me réveille	*I wake up*	je me lave	*I get washed*
je déjeune	*I have breakfast*	je rentre	*I come home*
je me déshabille	*I get undressed*	je me lève	*I get up*
je m'habille	*I get dressed*	je vais au collège	*I go to school*
je regarde la télé	*I watch TV*	je me couche	*I go to bed*
je fais mes devoirs	*I do my homework*	je promène le chien	*I walk the dog*

See also Time, Reflexive verbs

Days of the week and parts of the day

lundi	*Monday*	mardi	*Tuesday*
mercredi	*Wednesday*	jeudi	*Thursday*
vendredi	*Friday*	samedi	*Saturday*
dimanche	*Sunday*		

le jour	*day*	midi	*midday/noon*
la journée	*daytime*	la nuit	*night*
l'après-midi	*afternoon*	tous les jours	*every day*
le matin	*morning*	le soir	*evening*

Demonstrative adjectives

Use these when you want to talk about something in particular. In English, you'd use 'this', 'that', 'these', 'those': *this* girl, *those* men.

ce cahier (masculine)	*this/that exercise book*
cet homme (masculine)	*this/that man*
cette ville (feminine)	*this/that town*
ces animaux (plural)	*these/those animals*

You use *cet* for masculine nouns that begin with a vowel or a silent **h**. This makes them easier to say: *cet* arbre (*this/that tree*).

Demonstratives are **adjectives**, so remember to make them **agree**!

If you really want to make the difference between 'this/these' and 'that/those', just add **–ci** (*here*) and **–là** (*there*).

Ce cheval – ci est blanc, mais ce cheval – là est noir. (*This horse is white, but that horse is black.*)

See also — Adjectives

Directions

tournez à droite	*turn right*	tournez à gauche	*turn left*
allez/continuez tout droit	*go/carry straight on*		

prenez la première (rue)   à droite   *take the first (street) on the right*
          deuxième   à gauche   *second   left*
             troisième, etc.   *third, etc.*

avant (le pont)   *before (the bridge)*   après (le café)   *after (the café)*
à côté (du cinéma)   *next to (the cinema)*

See also — Numbers – cardinal and ordinal

Drink

le café	(black) coffee	le café-crème	white coffee
le chocolat chaud	hot chocolate	le jus d'orange	orange juice
l'eau minérale	mineral water	l'orangina	Orangina
le vin rouge	red wine	le cidre	cider
le thé au lait	tea (with milk)	le thé au citron	lemon tea
le lait chaud	hot milk	le citron pressé	fresh lemon juice
le coca	coca-cola	le vin blanc	white wine
le sirop de menthe	mint-cordial drink	la bière	beer

Also:

l'apéritif	pre-meal drink	le glaçon	ice-cube

See also Eating out

Eating out

Places to eat

le restaurant	restaurant	le bistro	bistro
la pizzeria	pizzeria	le café	café
le restaurant rapide	fast-food restaurant	la brasserie	(informal) restaurant

People

le garçon	waiter
le chef	chef
la serveuse	waitress
le caissier/la caissière	till-operator
le patron/la patronne	owner
le client/la cliente	customer

General

le menu (à prix fixe)	(fixed-price) menu
la carte	individually-priced menu
le couvert	cover charge
l'addition	bill

Continued overleaf

le pourboire		tip	
le choix		choice	
(non)-compris		(not) included	
le hors d'œuvre		starter	
le plat principal		main course	
le dessert		dessert	
sur la terrasse		on the terrace/outside	
le plat du jour		dish of the day	
la spécialité du pays		local speciality	
la cuisine (indienne)		(Indian) food	

Environment

le monde	world	la nature	nature
le soleil	sun	l'énergie (f.)	energy
le climat	climate	la circulation	traffic
la planète	planet	la terre	earth
l'écosystème (m.)	ecosystem	la pluie acide	acid rain
la couche d'ozone	ozone layer	la pollution urbaine	urban pollution
l'effet de serre (m.)	global warming	l'environnement (m.)	environment

See also Home area

Family

Immediate

le père	father	papa	dad
le fils	son	la sœur	sister
le demi-frère	half-brother	la demi-sœur	half-sister
la mère	mother	maman	mum
la fille	daughter	les parents (m.)	parents
le frère jumeau	twin brother	la sœur jumelle	twin sister

| la femme | wife | le mari | husband |
| le frère | brother | les enfants | children |

Extended

le grand-père	grandfather	l'oncle (m.)	uncle
la grand-mère	grandmother	la tante	aunt
le neveu	nephew	la nièce	niece
le cousin/la cousine	cousin		
les petits-enfants (m.)	grandchildren		
les grands-parents (m.)	grandparents		

Food

le pain	bread	le gâteau	cake
le lait	milk	le miel	honey
le riz	rice	le chocolat	chocolate
la baguette	French stick	le beurre	butter
le sucre	sugar	les œufs (m.)	eggs
les pâtes (f.)	pasta	les chips (m.)	crisps
le croissant	croissant	la confiture	jam
le fromage	cheese	l'huile (f.)	oil
le yaourt	yoghurt	les bonbons (m.)	sweets

la viande	meat	le biftek	steak
le poisson	fish	le jambon	ham
le saucisson	salami	les moules (f.)	mussels
le poulet	chicken	les saucisses (f.)	sausages
les fruits de mer	seafood		

la salade	lettuce	l'ail (m.)	garlic
le chou	cabbage	les tomates (f.)	tomatoes
les carottes (f.)	carrots	le chou-fleur	cauliflower
les petits pois (m.)	peas	les oignons (m.)	onions
les brocolis (m.)	broccoli	le champignon	mushroom
les frites (f.)	chips		
les pommes de terre (f.)	potatoes		
les choux de Bruxelles (m.)	Brussels sprouts		

Continued overleaf

la pomme	apple	la poire	pear
la banane	banana	la pêche	peach
l'orange (f.)	orange	le citron	lemon
la cerise	cherry	la fraise	strawberry
l'ananas (m.)	pineapple	le raisin	grape
le pamplemousse	grapefruit	la framboise	raspberry

See also Eating out, Meals, Shopping

Free time – at home

les cartes (f.)	cards	le dessin	drawing
la télévision	television	l'ordinateur (m.)	computer
les échecs (m.)	chess	la lecture	reading

la photographie	photography
le jeu de société	board game
le jeu électronique	computer game

Free time – going out

Places to go

le cinéma	cinema	le stade	sports stadium
la piscine	swimming pool	la patinoire	ice rink
la discothèque	disco	la boîte	disco/club
le théâtre	theatre	le centre sportif	sports centre
le bowling	bowling alley	le jardin public	park
le club des jeunes	youth club	la boum	party

Activities

la pêche	fishing	le vélo	cycling
la randonnée	walking/hiking	le shopping	shopping

Sporting Activities see Sport

Friends

l'ami (m.)	friend (boy)	l'amie (f.)	friend (girl)
le petit ami	boyfriend	la petite amie	girlfriend
le correspondant	penfriend (boy)	la correspondante	penfriend (girl)
le copain (m.)	friend/mate	la copine (f.)	friend/mate

See also Appearance, Personality

Future tense – Immediate

This future tense is used a lot in conversation. Use it when you are **going** to do something in the near future (just as you would in English).

You use the present tense of *aller* + infinitive

Je vais écouter de la musique.   *I'm going to listen to some music.*

Future tense – Standard

This is the 'proper' future tense and you use it when you would say **will** in English. (I will do my homework tomorrow.)

Here is the formula:

regular verb infinitive (stem) (for *–re* verbs, take off the *–e* first) + endings *– ai, – as, – a, – ons, – ez, – ont* = future tense

	–er manger	–ir choisir	–re vendre → vendr–
je	mangerai	choisirai	vendrai
tu	mangeras	choisiras	vendras
il/elle	mangera	choisira	vendra
nous	mangerons	choisirons	vendrons
vous	mangerez	choisirez	vendrez
ils/elles	mangeront	choisiront	vendront

Continued overleaf

Some irregular verbs are very common, and they have irregular stems in the future tense (although they still use the same endings).

infinitive	stem	future	infinitive	stem	future
être	ser–	je serai	avoir	aur–	j'aurai
aller	ir–	j'irai	faire	fer–	je ferai
devoir	devr–	je devrai	pouvoir	pourr–	je pourrai
vouloir	voudr–	je voudrai	savoir	saur–	je saurai
voir	verr–	je verrai	venir	viendr–	je viendrai

Exam tip

Make sure you learn these irregular verbs.

Gender

In French, all nouns are either **masculine** or **feminine**. (This is known as **gender**.) You will need to know the gender of nouns as this affects other words that are used with them (see **Agreement**).

Exam tip

Try to learn the gender of a noun at the same time as you learn the actual word.

In the dictionary, nouns will have (m.) or (f.) after them to indicate the gender.

the (masculine) = *le*
le chien   *the dog*
le stylo   *the pen*

the (feminine) = *la*
la souris   *the mouse*
la chambre   *the bedroom*

If a noun starts with a vowel or a silent **h**, use **l'** instead, to make it easier to say.

   l'arbre (m.)   *the tree*   l'église (f.)   *the church*

Both masculine and feminine nouns use *les* (the) when they are **plural**.

les magasins (m.) *the shops*   les rues (f.) *the streets*

a (masculine) = *un*
un village   *a village*
un frère   *a brother*

a (feminine) = *une*
une ville   *a town*
une sœur   *a sister*

Both masculine and feminine nouns use **des** (some/any) when they are **plural**.

As-tu des frères ou des sœurs?   *Have you any brothers or sisters?*

(We often miss out **some** in English, but you **must** put in **des** in French.)

> **See also**   Nouns

Giving orders (imperative)

When you are telling someone what to do, use the **tu** or **vous** part of the verb in the present tense (without *tu/vous*). With *–er* verbs, you leave off the last *–s* in the **tu** form.

Tournez à droite.	*Turn right.*	Traversez le pont.	*Cross the bridge.*
Vas-y!	*Go on!*	Ferme la porte. (tu)	*Close the door.*

Reflexive verbs need an extra pronoun after the imperative:

Levez-vous!	*Stand up!*	Taisez-vous!	*Be quiet!*
Réveille-toi!	*Wake up!*	Dépêche-toi!	*Hurry up!*

Going out, making arrangements

D'accord.	*OK.*	Je veux bien.	*I'd love to.*
Désolé, mais ...	*Sorry, but ...*	Je ne peux pas.	*I can't.*
Si on sortait?	*Shall we go out?*	A demain.	*See you tomorrow.*

Qu'est-ce que tu fais ce soir?   *What are you doing this evening?*
J'ai envie de ...   *I'd like to/I fancy doing ...*
J'ai envie d'aller au cinéma   *I fancy going to the cinema.*
On se retrouve/revoit où?   *Where shall we meet?*
On se retrouve/revoit à quelle heure?   *What time shall we meet?*
Ça commence à quelle heure?   *What time does it start?*
A ce soir.   *See you this evening.*
A samedi/dimanche, etc.   *See you Saturday/Sunday, etc.*

> **See also**   Free time – going out

Health

Qu'est-ce qui ne va pas?		What's the matter?	
Je ne me sens pas en forme.		I don't feel well.	
J'ai mal à …		It hurts me (somewhere).	
J'ai mal à la tête.		I've got a headache.	
J'ai mal à la gorge.		I've got a sore throat.	
J'ai mal au dos.		My back hurts.	
J'ai mal aux dents.		I've got toothache.	
J'ai mal au cœur.		I feel sick.	
Je suis enrhumé.		I've got a cold.	
J'ai la grippe.		I've got flu.	
le mal de mer	*sea-sickness*	le rhume des foins	*hay-fever*
diabétique	*diabetic*	allergique à	*allergic to*
végétarien	*vegetarian*	sain	*healthy*
en bonne santé	*in good health*	en pleine forme	*very fit*
chez le docteur	*at the doctor's*	chez le dentiste	*at the dentist's*
le cabinet	*the surgery*	le rendez-vous	*appointment*
le médicament	*medicine*	l'ordonnance	*prescription*

See also   Body

Holidays

les vacances	*holidays*	le voyage	*journey*
l'aéroport	*airport*	le passeport	*passport*
l'hôtel	*hotel*	le camping	*campsite*
la traversée	*crossing (ferry)*	la gare (routière)	*(coach) station*
le gîte	*holiday cottage*	au bord de la mer	*at the seaside*
à la montagne		*in the mountains*	
l'auberge de jeunesse		*youth hostel*	
le bureau de change		*currency exchange*	
les grandes vacances		*summer holidays*	
le bloc sanitaire	*toilet block*	le bac à vaisselle	*washing-up sink*
la chambre	*(hotel) room*	le sac à dos	*rucksack*

la tente	tent	l'emplacement	pitch
le bureau d'accueil	reception	l'ascenseur	lift

Je suis allé en vacances ...	I went on holiday ...
J'ai passé mes vacances ...	I spent my holidays ...
J'ai voyagé ...	I travelled ...
Je suis allé avec ...	I went with ...
Je suis resté chez ...	I stayed with ...

Home area

mon quartier	my area	près de chez moi	near where I live
en ville	in town	à la campagne	in the country
à la montagne	in the mountains	le centre-ville	town centre
au bord de la mer	by the seaside	la banlieue	suburbs
calme	quiet	industriel	industrial
propre	clean	sale	dirty
tranquille	peaceful	ennuyeux	boring
pollué	polluted	historique	historic
agréable	pleasant	animé	lively

See also Environment, Town

House and home

la maison	house	l'immeuble (m.)	block of flats
en bas	downstairs	en haut	upstairs
la ferme	farm	la cave	cellar
au premier étage	on the first floor	l'entrée (f.)	entrance hall
la cuisine	kitchen	le salon	lounge
l'escalier (m.)	staircase	la chambre	bedroom
les toilettes (f.)	toilet	la salle de jeux	play-room
le grenier	attic	le garage	garage
la buanderie	utility-room	le balcon	balcony
le jardin	garden	la salle de bains	bathroom

Continued overleaf

le bureau	*study*	le palier	*landing*
la véranda	*conservatory*	la terrasse	*patio*
la serre	*greenhouse*	le sous-sol	*basement*
la salle de séjour	*living-room*	la salle à manger	*dining-room*
au rez-de-chaussée	*on the ground floor*	l'appartement (m.)	*flat*

le lit	*bed*	la lampe	*lamp*
le rideau	*curtain*	l'armoire (f.)	*wardrobe*
le téléviseur	*TV set*	le tapis	*rug*
la chaîne compact	*stereo*	la commode	*chest of drawers*
le fauteuil	*armchair*	la moquette	*carpet*

Household jobs

Most of these use the verb **faire**

Je fais la vaisselle.	*I do the washing-up.*
J'essuie la vaisselle.	*I dry the dishes.*
Je fais la cuisine.	*I do the cooking.*
Je fais mon lit.	*I make my bed.*
Je range/nettoie ma chambre.	*I tidy/clean my room.*
Je fais le ménage.	*I do the housework.*
Je mets/débarrasse la table.	*I set/clear the table.*
Je passe l'aspirateur (m.).	*I do the hoovering.*
Je fais les courses.	*I do the shopping.*
Je fais du bricolage.	*I do odd jobs/DIY.*

Also useful:

bien rangé/mal rangé	*tidy/untidy*
Ma chambre est mal rangée	*My bedroom is untidy.*

Imperfect tense

You use the imperfect tense when talking about something in the past that **went on for a length of time** or that **used to happen regularly**. It's also used for **description** in the past, and for **interrupted** action. (You can recognise it in English by 'was/were doing' and 'used to'.)

Here is the formula: (the same for **all** verbs except **être**)

| **nous** form of the present tense *minus* the *–ons* (stem) | + | endings *–ais, –ais, –ait, –ions, –iez, –aient* | = | imperfect tense |

infinitive	stem	imperfect	
regarder	regard–	je regardais	I was watching/I used to watch
habiter	habit–	nous habitions	we were living/we used to live
avoir	av–	il y avait	there was/were/used to be
manger	mange–	ils mangeaient	they were eating/used to eat

être is the exception, since the present tense (**nous** form) does not end *–ons* (nous sommes).

The imperfect stem for **être** is **ét–**: C'était génial. *It was great.*

Jobs

Il/elle travaille ...   *he/she works ...*

dans un bureau	*in an office*	à la maison	*at home*
dans une école	*in a school*	dans une usine	*in a factory*
dans un magasin	*in a shop*	chez (Renault)	*for (Renault)*

le/la fonctionnaire	*civil servant*	l'infirmière (f.)	*nurse*
le/la réceptionniste	*receptionist*	l'électricien (m.)	*electrician*
le fermier	*farmer*	le/la concierge	*caretaker*
le docteur	*doctor*	le/la secrétaire	*secretary*
le/la professeur	*teacher*	la vendeuse	*sales assistant*
le garagiste	*garage owner*	le mécanicien	*mechanic*
le maçon	*builder*	le policier	*policeman*
le pompier	*firefighter*	le facteur	*postman*
l'ingénieur (m.)	*engineer*		

l'employé(e) (m.,f.)	*employee*
l'informaticien(ne) (m.,f.)	*computer scientist*
le/la technicien(ne)	*technician*
l'ouvrier/l'ouvrière (m.,f.)	*manual worker*
le chauffeur d'autobus	*bus driver*

Letters

You are more likely to write **informal letters** (e.g. to a penfriend).

Begin with:	Cher/Chère (m.,f.) ...	*Dear ...*
End with:	Amitiés	*Best wishes*
	Grosses bises	*Love from ... (big hugs!)*
	Je t'embrasse	*Love and kisses*

It all depends how well you know your penfriend!

Formal letters start: Monsieur/Madame   *Dear Sir/Madam*

and end: Je vous prie d'agréer, Monsieur/Madame, l'expression de mes sentiments les plus respectueux.

(Don't ask! This is as close as you'll get to 'Yours faithfully'!)

Link words

Apart from the obvious ones, link words can make a big difference to your writing style. They can also help you plan your way through a sequence of events when writing a story.

et	*and*	puis	*then*
mais	*but*	ensuite	*next*
d'abord	*first of all*	finalement	*finally*
après	*after*	enfin	*at last*

Meals

le petit déjeuner	*breakfast*	le goûter	*afternoon snack*
le repas du soir	*evening meal*	le dîner	*dinner*
le casse-croûte	*snack*	le pique-nique	*picnic*
le déjeuner	*lunch/midday meal*	le plat à emporter	*take-away meal*

See also   Eating out, Food, Snacks

Media – general

le cinéma	*cinema*	la radio	*radio*
le théâtre	*theatre*	la télévision	*television*
la presse	*press*	le journal	*newspaper*
le quotidien	*daily paper*	l'hebdomadaire (m.)	*weekly paper*
la maison de la presse	*newsagent*		
les titres (m.)	*headlines*		

See also Opinions

Money

le billet	*bank note*	la livre sterling	*pound (£) sterling*
la monnaie	*change*	la pièce	*coin*
l'argent (m.) (de poche)	*(pocket) money*	le franc	*franc*

Ça coûte combien? — *How much does it cost?*
Ça coûte ... — *It costs ...*

Months of the year and seasons

Months

janvier	*January*	février	*February*
mars	*March*	avril	*April*
mai	*May*	juin	*June*
juillet	*July*	août	*August*
septembre	*September*	octobre	*October*
novembre	*November*	décembre	*December*

Exam tip

Remember – names of months start with a small letter in French.

Continued overleaf

Seasons

le printemps	spring	l'été (m.)	summer
l'automne (m.)	autumn	l'hiver (m.)	winter
au printemps	in spring	en été	in summer
en automne	in autumn	en hiver	in winter

Music

la musique pop	pop music	le rock	rock
la chaîne stéréo	stereo system	le jazz	jazz
le rap	rap	la platine laser	CD player
la cassette (K7)*	cassette		

le magnétophone	cassette recorder
la musique folklorique	folk music
le baladeur/le walkman	walkman
la musique classique	classical music
le disque compact/CD	CD

*They are often called these in discographies – try saying it! (in French)

Nationality

anglais	English	espagnol	Spanish
écossais	Scottish	néerlandais	Dutch
autrichien(ne)	Austrian	français	French
irlandais	Irish	italien(ne)	Italian
suédois	Swedish	allemand	German
gallois	Welsh	belge	Belgian
suisse	Swiss	grec/grecque	Greek

Exam tip

Remember – these are adjectives and have to agree with the noun.

See also

Countries

Negatives

This is when you say **not** in English. (I **don't** care. You **can't** play.)

To make a negative statement in French, you put *ne* in front of the **verb** and *pas* after it.

Here is the formula:

ne/n' + **verb** + **pas**

Je **ne** suis **pas** prêt.   *I'm not ready.*
Il **n'**a **pas** de frères.   *He hasn't any brothers.*

Using the negative can affect whatever comes after it. ***Un, une, du, de la, de l'*** and ***des*** all change to ***de*** or ***d'*** in the negative.

Je n'ai pas d'animaux.   *I haven't got any pets.*
Nous ne faisons pas de judo.   *We're not doing judo.*

In the **perfect tense**, *ne* and *pas* go before and after the **auxiliary** verb and the past participle goes after *pas*.

Here is the formula:

ne + **auxiliary (*avoir/être*)** + **pas** + **past participle**

Je n'ai pas lu ce livre.
(*I haven't read that book*)

There are other negative expressions apart from ***ne ... pas*** which work the same way.

Two useful ones are:

ne ... jamais (never)   Je **ne** mange **jamais** de viande.   *I never eat meat.*

ne ... plus (no longer/more)   Il **n'**a **plus** de pêches.   *He has no more peaches.*

Nouns

The most important thing about nouns (naming words) in French – apart from the actual meaning of the words – is their **gender**. This can affect other words that are used with them, e.g. adjectives.

See also   Gender

Numbers – cardinal and ordinal

Cardinal

1 un, une	11 onze	21 vingt et un	80 quatre-vingts
2 deux	12 douze	22 vingt-deux	81 quatre-vingt-un
3 trois	13 treize	30 trente	90 quatre-vingt-dix
4 quatre	14 quatorze	31 trente et un	91 quatre-vingt-onze
5 cinq	15 quinze	40 quarante	100 cent
6 six	16 seize	50 cinquante	101 cent un
7 sept	17 dix-sept	60 soixante	150 cent cinquante
8 huit	18 dix-huit	70 soixante-dix	200 deux cents
9 neuf	19 dix-neuf	71 soixante et onze	1 000 mille
10 dix	20 vingt	72 soixante-douze	1 000 000 un million

Ordinal

premier, première	*first*	deuxième	*second*
troisième	*third*	quatrième	*fourth*
cinquième	*fifth*	sixième	*sixth*

*When saying the date in French, just give the **cardinal** number – e.g. le treize mars. The only exception is the **first** of the month: *le premier.*

le premier janvier   le premier mai

Object pronouns – direct and indirect

These are words in English like **me, you, him, her, it, us, them**. They refer to people or things that are affected by the action of the verb. (I saw **her** but she didn't see **me**.)

Direct object pronouns

The **direct** object pronoun refers to the person or thing which has an action done to it.

In French, these are: *me, te, le, la, nous, vous, les*

	singular		plural	
1st person	me/m'	me	nous	us
2nd person	te/t'	you	vous	you
3rd person	le/l', la/l'	him/he/it	les	them

In French, the **direct object pronoun goes before the verb**.

Il **me** regarde.   *He's watching me.*   Je **l'**attends.   *I'm waiting for him.*

Indirect object pronouns

Indirect object pronouns refer to people or things which are not directly affected by the action of the verb. In English, you often find the word **to** used with them. (I sent (**to**) him a postcard. He spoke **to** me.)
In French, these are: *me, te, lui, nous, vous, leur*.

	singular		plural	
1st person	me	*to me*	nous	*to us*
2nd person	te	*to you*	vous	*to you*
3rd person	lui	*to him/her/it*	leur	*to them*

In French, **indirect object pronouns go before the verb**.
Elle **lui** donne un cadeau. (*She gives him/her a present.*)

Opinions

A mon avis	*In my opinion*	Je trouve/pense que …	*I think that …*
C'est/C'était …	*It's/It was …*	Ça m'énerve	*It gets on my nerves*
super	*brilliant*	génial	*great*
cool	*good/cool*	pas mal	*not bad/OK*
ennuyeux	*boring*	barbant	*boring*
affreux	*awful*	nul	*terrible*

Participles

The **past participle** is the second bit of compound tenses like the perfect and the pluperfect. (See the separate sections on these.) It tells you **what** has been happening, and is usually formed from the **infinitive**.

Use **en** + **present participle** if you want to express the idea of 'while do**ing**' or 'by do**ing**' something.

Here is the formula for the present participles:

| **nous** form of the verb in the present tense minus –**ons** (stem) | + | ending –**ant** | = | present participle |

regarder → nous regardons → regard– + –ant = regardant

en regardant — *while watching*
Anne s'est endormie en regardant la télé. — *Anne fell asleep while watching TV.*

You can only use this structure when the subject of the two verbs is the same. (**Anne** was watching TV and **Anne** fell asleep.)

See also — Perfect tense, Pluperfect tense

Past tense – general

There are several past tenses in French, but you are only likely to use three of them.

The most common one is the **perfect** tense which is used for **completed actions in the past**. This is the one you use for stories and saying what happened at the weekend/on holiday, etc. (It translates as 'did', 'has done' in English.)

The **pluperfect** tense goes further back in the past to what **had** happened. (He **had** injured his foot so he couldn't play football.)

Both the perfect and pluperfect tenses are **compound** tenses, i.e. they are made up of two bits: an auxiliary verb and a past participle.

The **imperfect** tense is used when you want to say what someone **used** to do, or what someone **was** do**ing**.

Exam tip
See the separate sections on each of these three tenses.

See also
Tense – general

Perfect tense

The **perfect** tense is a **compound** tense, so it is made up of two parts: the **auxiliary** and the **past participle**.

- The **auxiliary** (helping verb) is the present tense of *avoir* or *être* (usually *avoir*). It goes with the **subject** and shows **who** or **what** is doing the action of the verb.

- The **past participle** is usually formed from the **infinitive** and shows **what** has been happening.

Here is the formula for the past participle of regular verbs:

–er verbs:	Take off the *–er* and add *é*.	donner → donn– + é	= donné
–ir verbs:	just take of the *–r*.	finir → fini–	= fini
–re verbs:	Take off the *–re* and add *u*.	vendre → vend– + u	= vendu

Perfect tense with *avoir*

(Most verbs in French go with *avoir*.)

donner	finir	vendre
j'ai donné	j'ai fini	j'ai vendu
tu as donné	tu as fini	tu as vendu
il/elle a donné	il/elle a fini	il/elle a vendu
nous avons donné	nous avons fini	nous avons vendu
vous avez donné	vous avez fini	vous avez vendu
ils/elles ont donné	ils/elles ont fini	ils/elles ont vendu

Continued overleaf

Here are some **avoir** verbs with **irregular** past participles.

avoir	eu	j'ai eu	*I had*
devoir	dû	j'ai dû	*I should have*
voir	vu	j'ai vu	*I saw*
mettre	mis	j'ai mis	*I put (on)*
dire	dit	j'ai dit	*I said*
être	été	j'ai été	*I've been*
boire	bu	j'ai bu	*I drank*
lire	lu	j'ai lu	*I read*
vouloir	voulu	j'ai voulu	*I wanted*
prendre	pris	j'ai pris	*I took*
écrire	écrit	j'ai écrit	*I wrote*
faire	fait	j'ai fait	*I did*

Perfect tense with être

Some verbs go with **être**. There are not many of these and they are nearly all regular, so the past participle is regular too.

But – with **être** verbs, the past participle **agrees** with the subject.

Marianne est allée en ville. *Marianne went into town.*
Mes frères sont restés à la maison. *My brothers stayed at home.*

Here are the most common **être** verbs. They tend to be verbs of motion and you may find it helpful to learn them in pairs.

aller	*to go*	venir	*to come*
arriver	*to arrive*	partir	*to leave/depart*
entrer	*to go in*	sortir	*to go out*
rester	*to stay*	tomber	*to fall*
monter	*to go up*	descendre	*to go down*
naître*	*to be born*	mourir*	*to die*

* These two have **irregular** past participles:

naître	né	je suis né	*I was born*
mourir	mort	elle est morte	*she died*

Reflexive verbs also take **être** in the perfect tense.
Nous nous sommes levés à huit heures. *We got up at eight o'clock.*

See also Past tense – general, Participles, Agreement

Personality

bavard	talkative	sympa(thique)	nice
timide	shy	travailleur/euse	hard-working
charmant	charming	sage	well-behaved
marrant	funny	gentil(le)	kind
habile	skilful	maladroit	clumsy
sérieux/se	serious	têtu	stubborn
paresseux/se	lazy	sportif/ve	sporty
drôle	funny	pénible	a pain
étourdi	scatty	méchant	naughty

Pluperfect tense

You use the **pluperfect tense** to say what **had** happened in the past (before something else happened).

The pluperfect tense is a **compound** tense like the perfect tense. It is formed just like the perfect tense, except that the **auxiliary** verb (*avoir* or *être*) is in the **imperfect** tense, and not the present tense.

Elle avait acheté un livre.   She had bought a book.
Nous étions arrivés la veille.   We had arrived the previous day.

Past participles agree with subjects when you use *être* verbs in the pluperfect tense, just as they do in the perfect tense.

See also   Past tense – general

Plurals

With plural nouns, masculine and feminine, you don't need to think about **gender** when saying **the** and **some/any**.

les (m.) and (f.)	the	les garçons (m.) les chaises (f.)
des (m.) and (f.)	some/any	des pommes (f.) des animaux (m.)

You make most French nouns plural by adding *–s* (like you would in English), but there are some exceptions:

- Nouns that end *–al* become *–aux*   un cheval   des chevaux
- Nouns that end *–au, –eau, – eu* add *–x*   un château   des châteaux
- Nouns that end *–s, –x, –z* stay the same   une souris   des souris

This one is very weird!

un œil   *an eye*   des yeux   *eyes*

Possessive adjectives

These tell you who something belongs to (my, your, his, her, our, their in English).

They are adjectives, so in French they have to **agree** with the noun they relate to.

masculine	feminine	plural	
mon	ma	mes	*my*
ton	ta	tes	*your* (tu)
son	sa	ses	*his/ her/ its*
notre	notre	nos	*our*
votre	votre	vos	*your* (vous)
leur	leur	leurs	*their*

See also   Adjectives

Prepositions

These words tell you where things are.

sur	*on*	devant	*in front of*	à côté de	*next to*
sous	*under*	derrière	*behind*	en face de	*opposite*
dans	*in*	entre	*between*	en	*in*
chez	*at the house of*				

- **de** combines with **le** and **les** to make two new words.

Here is the rule:

de + le = du	en face du cinéma	*opposite the cinema*
de + la = de la	à côté de la gare	*next to the station*
de + l' = de l'	à côté de l'église	*next to the church*
de + les = des	en face des magasins	*opposite the shops*

- **à** means **to** and also combines with **le** and **les** to make new words.

Here is the rule:

à + le = au	Il va au stade	*He goes to the stadium*
à + la = à la	Je vais à la banque	*I go to the bank*
à + l' = à l'	Nous allons à l'hôtel	*We go to the hotel*
à + les = aux	Ils vont aux Pays-Bas	*They go to the Netherlands*

Present tense

The **infinitive** (name or title of a verb) is what you will find if you look up a verb in the dictionary, but you can't use it with a subject!

There are two kinds of verbs: regular and irregular. **Regular** verbs follow a set pattern (see below). **Irregular** verbs don't, and you'll need to learn the most common ones off by heart.

There are three types of **regular** verbs: *–er* (jouer), *–ir* (finir) and *–re* (vendre). Here's what you do to make the present tense:

Start with the infinitive	→	Take off the last two letters (stem)	→	Add the endings [according to the subject] (a different set for each type)

–er	–ir	–re
jouer (infinitive)	finir (infinitive)	vendre (infinitive)
jou– (stem)	fin– (stem)	vend– (stem)
je jou**e**	je fin**is**	je vend**s**
tu jou**es**	tu fin**is**	tu vend**s**
il/elle jou**e**	il/elle fin**it**	il/elle vend (no ending)
nous jou**ons**	nous fin**issons**	nous vend**ons**
vous jou**ez**	vous fin**issez**	vous vend**ez**
ils/elles jou**ent**	ils/elles fin**issent**	ils/elles vend**ent**

Continued overleaf

Here are some **irregular** verbs that you can't manage without!

être (*to be*)	avoir (*to have*)	aller (*to go*)	faire (*to do/make*)
je suis	j'ai	je vais	je fais
tu es	tu as	tu vas	tu fais
il/elle est	il/elle a	il/elle va	il/elle fait
nous sommes	nous avons	nous allons	nous faisons
vous êtes	vous avez	vous allez	vous faites
ils/elles sont	ils/elles ont	ils/elles vont	ils/elles font

Problems – adolescent

les parents (m.)	*parents*	les boutons (m.)	*spots*
le travail	*job*	l'absentéisme	*truancy*
les brutalités	*bullying*	la peau	*skin*
le chômage	*unemployment*	les examens (m.)	*exams*
la colle	*detention*	la drogue	*drug*
le SIDA	*Aids*	la mode	*fashion*

Questions

General

You can make a question in two ways:

- Turn round the subject and verb.

Quel âge **as-tu**? *How old are you*? (When you do this, a hyphen goes between the verb and subject.)

- Put ***Est-ce que/qu'*** in front of your original statement.

Est-ce que vous avez fini?   *Have you finished?*

Specific

Qui?	*Who?*	Qu'est-ce que?	*What?*
Quand?	*When?*	Où?	*Where?*
A quelle heure?	*What time?*	Quel/Quelle?	*Which?*
Pourquoi?	*Why?*	Comment?	*How?*

Reading material

le livre	book	la BD	comic book
le quotidien	daily paper	le roman	novel
la revue	magazine	le journal	newspaper
le magazine	magazine	l'hebdomadaire (m.)	weekly paper

Reflexive verbs

You use these verbs when you are doing something to **yourself** (washing, getting up, etc.). The action is **reflected back** to the subject. In French, there is an extra pronoun between the subject and the verb.

se laver	to get washed
je me lave	I get washed
tu te laves	you get washed
il/elle se lave	he/she gets washed
nous nous lavons	we get washed
vous vous lavez	you get washed
ils/elles se lavent	they get washed

Here are some useful reflexive verbs:

se réveiller	*to wake up*
se doucher	*to have a shower*
se déshabiller	*to get undressed*
se promener	*to go for a walk*
se lever	*to get up*
s'habiller	*to get dressed*
se coucher	*to go to bed*
se dépêcher	*to hurry up*

Reflexive verbs take **être** as the auxiliary in the perfect tense. So you must remember to make the past participle agree with the subject!

Je me suis couché(e) à onze heures. *I went to bed at eleven o'clock.*
Bernadette s'est levée très tard. *Bernadette got up very late.*
Nous nous sommes promenés en ville. *We went for a walk in town.*

Relative pronouns

These are the words *qui* and *que*, and they mean **who**, **which** and **that**. They can refer to both people and things.

In the relative clause, *qui* is the **subject** of the verb and *que* is the **direct object** of the verb.

La dame **qui** traverse la rue.	*The lady who is crossing the road.* (subject)
Le garçon **que** j'ai rencontré.	*The boy (whom) I met.* (object)
Le chat **qui** a attrapé la souris.	*The cat which caught the mouse.* (subject)
Les baskets **que** j'ai achetées.	*The trainers that I bought.* (object)

School

l'élève (m.,f.)	*pupil*
le directeur/la directrice	*headteacher (m./f.)*
le/la concierge	*caretaker*
le conseiller/la conseillère d'orientation	*careers officer*
le bureau	*office*
le couloir	*corridor*
l'infirmerie (f.)	*sick bay*
le CDI	*resource centre*
le gymnase	*gym*
la (grande) salle	*(main) hall*
la salle de permanence	*study room*
le terrain de sport	*sports field*
le français	*French*
l'espagnol (m.)	*Spanish*
les mathématiques/maths (f.)	*maths*
la biologie	*biology*
la physique	*physics*
l'histoire (f.)	*history*
EPS	*PE*
le dessin	*art*
l'art dramatique (m.)	*drama*

la récréation	*breaktime*
les devoirs (m.)	*homework*
l'emploi du temps (m.)	*timetable*
les vacances (f.)	*holidays*
l'examen (m.)	*exam*
le copain/la copine	*(school) friend*
le/la secrétaire	*secretary*
la cantine	*dining hall*
la cour	*playground*
la bibliothèque	*library*
le laboratoire	*laboratory*
la piscine	*swimming-pool*
la salle de classe	*classroom*
la salle des profs	*staffroom*
les vestiaires (m.)	*changing-rooms*
l'Anglais (m.)	*English*
l'Allemand (m.)	*German*
l'Espagnol	*Spanish*
l'informatique (f.)	*ITC*
la chimie	*Chemistry*
les sciences (f.)	*science*
la géographie/géo	*geography*
EMT	*technology*
la musique	*music*
le dessin	*art*
la matière	*subject*
l'assemblée (f.)	*assembly*
la colle	*detention*
le trimestre	*term*
la rentrée	*back to school*
les notes (f.)	*marks*

Seasons *see Months of the year and seasons*

Shopping

le magasin	*shop*
la boutique	*small shop*
le marché	*market*
le grand magasin	*department store*
le supermarché	*supermarket*
l'hypermarché (m.)	*hypermarket*
la boulangerie	*baker's*
la pâtisserie	*cake shop*
l'épicerie (f.)	*grocer's*
l'alimentation (f.)	*minimarket*
la boucherie	*butcher's*
la charcuterie	*pork butcher's, deli*
la crémerie	*dairy products*
la fromagerie	*cheese shop*
la poissonnerie	*fish shop*
la quincaillerie	*ironmonger's*
la droguerie	*hardware shop*
la confiserie	*sweet shop*
la pharmacie	*chemist's*
la papeterie	*stationer's*
la librairie	*book shop*
le tabac	*tobacconist's*
le rayon	*department*
la caisse	*check-out*
le prix	*price*
la vitrine	*shop window*
le sous-sol	*basement*
la marque	*brand name*
l'ascenseur (m.)	*lift*
le rez-de-chaussée	*ground floor*
Ça fait combien?	*How much?*
Quelle taille?	*What size?*
Je voudrais ...	*I'd like ...*
Je peux l'essayer?	*Can I try it on?*

See also Town, Money

Snacks

un sandwich	*sandwich*	une glace	*ice-cream*
un beignet	*doughnut*	une omelette	*omelette*
une merguez	*spicy sausage*	un hot dog	*hot dog*
un croque-monsieur			*toasted cheese and ham sandwich*
une portion de frites			*portion of chips*

See also Eating out, Food

Some, any (partitive)

You use this when you want to refer to an unspecified part of something instead of the whole thing. (We sometimes leave it out in English, but in French you have to put it in.)

Je voudrais du café.	*I'd like some coffee.*
Je ne prends pas de sucre.	*I don't take sugar.*
J'ai des pommes et des oranges.	*I've got apples and oranges.*

Here is the rule:

de + le = du	Avez-vous du beurre?	*Have you any butter?*
de + la = de la	Tu veux de la salade?	*Do you want some salad?*
de + l' = de l'	Je voudrais de l'eau.	*I'd like some water.*
de + les = des	As-tu des frères ou des soeurs?	*Have you got any brothers or sisters?*
	Avez-vous des timbres?	*Have you got any stamps?*

In a **negative** sentence, all partitives revert to ***de/d'***.

Il n'y a pas de fromage.	*There isn't any cheese.*
Je ne mange pas de viande.	*I don't eat meat.*
Nous n'avons pas d'animaux.	*We haven't any pets.*
Je ne veux pas de sel.	*I don't want any salt.*
Elle n'a pas de frères.	*She hasn't got any brothers.*

Sport

le foot/football	football	le handball	handball
l'équitation (f.)	horse riding	la natation	swimming
la gymnastique	gymnastics	la pêche	fishing
le patin à glace	ice-skating	le rugby	rugby
le volley	volleyball	la voile	sailing
l'athlétisme	athletics	la boxe	boxing
le ski	skiing	le tennis	tennis
le cyclisme	cycling	le basket	basketball
le cricket	cricket	l'escrime (f.)	fencing
le patin à roulettes	roller-skating	le snooker	snooker

Subject pronouns

In English, these are the words **I, you, he, she, it, we** and **they**. They show **who** or **what** is doing the action of the verb.

je	I	1st person singular
tu	you	2nd person singular
il/elle	he/she/it	3rd person singular
nous	we	1st person plural
vous	you	2nd person plural
ils/elles	they	3rd person plural

Three things to remember!

- *je* becomes *j'* before a vowel or a silent **h**.   J'aime. *I like*
- *tu* (you) is **familiar** and always **singular**. *Vous* (you) can be used in the singular, too, but in a **polite** way, i.e. to someone you don't know. It is always used when talking to **more than one person**.
- The third person (singular and plural) often turns up in disguise as a **noun**. Learn to recognise it and don't get caught out!

Mes cousins habitent au Canada.   *My cousins live in Canada.*
Gérard aime jouer aux échecs.   *Gérard likes playing chess.*

Television

l'émission (f.)	programme	la météo	weather forecast
le jeu télévisé	game show	la causerie	chat show
la série policière	police series	le film comique	comedy film
le feuilleton	soap	la chaîne	channel
les publicités (f)	adverts	le dessin animé	cartoon

le reportage sportif	sports programme
les informations (f.)	the news
la pièce de théâtre	play
le documentaire	documentary

Tense – general

Tense is just a grammatical way of saying **time**. The tense you use for a verb shows **when** the action took place.

There are three basic kinds of tense: **past**, **present** and **future**. The present and future tenses are quite straightforward, but there are several different past tenses and you need to be sure which one you want to use. (See **Past tense – general**.)

See also   under separate Tense headings

Tickets

le billet	ticket	le tarif réduit	reduced rate
la place	seat	l'entrée (f.)	entrance (cost)
l'adulte (m.,f.)	adult	l'aller-retour (m.)	return ticket
le guichet	ticket office	le tarif	cost
le tarif étudiant	student rate	le prix	price
le terrain	pitch/ground	l'enfant (m.,f.)	child
le billet simple	single ticket	le distributeur	ticket machine

See also   **Cinema, Transport**

Time

Quelle heure est-il?	What's the time?
Il est une heure	It's one o'clock
Il est deux heures	It's 2 o'clock
Il est midi	It's midday
Il est minuit	It's midnight
Il est seize heures	It's 4.00 p.m.
... et demie	half past
... et quart	quarter past
... moins le quart	quarter to
Il est midi et demi	It's 12.30 (day)
Il est six heures cinq	It's 06.05
Il est cinq heures vingt	It's 05.20
Il est neuf heures moins vingt-cinq	It's twenty-five to nine (08.35)
Il est vingt et une heures trente (21h 30)	It's half past nine p.m.

Town

la ville	town
l'hôtel (m.)	hotel
le port	port
le château	castle
l'école (f.)	school
le musée	museum
l'aéroport	airport
la piscine	swimming pool
la poste	post office
la bibliothèque	library
le théâtre	theatre
la banque	bank
la gare	railway station
l'église (f.)	church
le cinéma	cinema
l'hôpital (m.)	hospital
la patinoire	ice-rink
le centre-ville	town centre
le stade	sports stadium
la cathédrale	cathedral
le jardin public	park
le marché	market
le centre commercial	shopping centre
l'agence de voyages (f.)	travel agency
le syndicat d'initiative	tourist office
l'auberge de jeunesse (f.)	youth hostel
la gare routière	bus/coach station
le commissariat de police	police station
le collège	secondary school

l'hôtel de ville/la mairie — town hall
l'office de tourisme — tourist office
la station-service — filling station

Transport

l'autobus (m.) — bus
le car — coach
l'hélicoptère (m.) — helicopter
le vélomoteur — moped
la voiture — car
l'aéroglisseur (m.) — hovercraft
le métro — underground/metro
le VTT (vélo tout terrain) — mountain bike
le train — train
le vélo — bike
le camion — lorry
l'avion (m.) — plane
la moto — motorbike

- Je voyage **en** train/**en** voiture, etc. — *I travel by train, by car, etc.*
  BUT
  Je voyage **à** cheval/**à** pied. — *I travel on horseback/on foot.*

Verbs

Verbs are the most important words in a sentence: they say what is happening.

A verb is listed in the dictionary under the **infinitive**. (This is the name or title of the verb.) You can't use the infinitive with the subject of the verb, so you need to learn the formula to get from the infinitive to the part of the verb which goes with the subject.

There are **two** types of verb: regular and irregular. **Regular** verbs follow a set pattern. **Irregular** verbs don't, and you will need to learn the most common ones off by heart.

Exam tip

You need to be able to use verbs confidently. This is where you will pick up valuable marks.

See also
Tense – General

Weather

la météo	*Weather*
Quel temps fait-il?	*What's the weather like?*
Il fait beau	*It's fine*
Il fait chaud	*It's hot*
Il fait froid	*It's cold*
Il y a du vent	*It's windy*
Il pleut	*It's raining*
Il neige	*It's snowing*
Il fait mauvais	*It's bad weather*
Il y a du soleil	*It's sunny*
Il y a des nuages	*It's cloudy*
Il y a du brouillard	*It's foggy*
Il y a de l'orage	*It's stormy*
Il gèle	*It's freezing*

If you want to say what the weather **was** like in the past tense, use the **imperfect** tense, since you are using description.

Il faisait chaud	*It was hot*
Il y avait du vent	*It was windy*
Il pleuvait	*It was raining*
Il neigeait	*It was snowing*

Work see Jobs